"IN MY FEELINGS"

an·thol·o·gy·col·lec·tion

OTHER BOOKS BY ROBERT M. DRAKE

Spaceship (2012)
The Great Artist (2012)
Science (2013)
Beautiful Chaos (2014)
Beautiful Chaos 2 (2014)
Black Butterfly (2015)
A Brilliant Madness (2015)
Beautiful and Damned (2016)
Broken Flowers (2016)
Gravity: A Novel (2017)
Star Theory (2017)
Chaos Theory (2017)
Light Theory (2017)
Moon Theory (2017)
Dead Pop Art (2017)
Chasing The Gloom: A Novel (2017)
Moon Matrix (2018)
Seeds of Wrath (2018)
Dawn of Mayhem (2018)
The King is Dead (2018)
What I Feel When I Don't Want To Feel (2019)
What I Say To Myself When I Need To Calm The Fuck Down (2019)
What I Say When I'm Not Saying A Damn Thing (2019)
What I Mean When I Say Miss You, Love You & Fuck You (2019)
What I Say To Myself When I Need To Walk Away, Let Go And Fucking Move On (2019)
What I Really Mean When I Say Good-bye, Don't Go And Leave Me The Fuck Alone (2019)
The Advice I Give Others But Fail To Practice My Damn Self (2019)
The Things I Feel In My Fucking Soul And The Things That Took Years To Understand (2019)
Something Broken, Something Beautiful (2020)

For Excerpts and Updates please follow:

Instagram.com/rmdrk
Facebook.com/rmdrk
Twitter.com/rmdrk

Book Cover: ROBERT M. DRAKE

For the broken For the beautiful
You know who you are

"IN MY FEELINGS"

ROBERT M. DRAKE

ANYMORE

It's sad.

Because

*you we're once
the only person*

*I would run to
and now,*

*I barely know
who you are*

anymore.

MORE THAN ONCE

Maybe we aren't
meant for this.

Maybe we're meant
for more.

So be patient
with what hurts

and smile
at what you've learned.

The process is beautiful.

If you don't trust it.
You'll go through it

again.

And nothing
is ever lost

but time is,
if the same love

is experienced
more than once.

US AND THEM

There is you.

Me.
Us.

And then,
there is them.

And none of us
want what we deserve.

None of us want
what belongs to us.

We just want
what we crave.

Even if it hurts.

Even if it
demoralizes us.

We love
what we love

and none of us
give a damn

of what kind of pain
it brings.

Because in the end,
how it hurts

does not matter.

All that matters is,
that we loved

the way we loved

and hope
it doesn't consume us.

Hope
it doesn't completely

destroy us.

And doesn't devour
our souls

in the mist
of all the things

we owe
to ourselves.

SCARS INSIDE

You trust
without building walls.

You love
as if you've never

been hurt.

And you give
without expecting anything

in return.

You're beautiful,
baby

but this is how
you get your heart broken.

This is how
you get scars

in your heart.

HOW TO LOVE

We don't even know
why we hurt

the way we hurt.

Love
the way we love.

Want
or care

the way we do.

We just do
because we must.

Because we feel.

Because this has been
the only way

we have learned
how to heal.

How to let go.
How to cry

and laugh

and most importantly,
how to love.

GIVE IT

Some people cut
so deep

that no amount of time
could ever heal you.

No amount of love
could ever make you

forget.

It's painful.
But it's the truth.

When it's real.
It's real.

And no one could ever
take that

away from you.

No one could ever
replace

the one you give
your heart to.

SPEAK TO YOU

That sad song
is your heart.

That movie that makes you cry
is your life.

And that story
you keep

re-reading is your love.

Everything you do
reminds you

of *that* special person.

That one person
who feels the same way.

Who relates
to all the things

that speak to you.

A CLUE

You're alive
but you're not living

your life.

The same way
you want to heal

and find self-love
but you don't have

the slightest clue
where to start.

Search within.

WITH DARKNESS

It's the way you remind me
to love myself.

The way
you make me feel.

The way
you bring out

certain things about me.

Even some
I've deeply forgotten.

You make me remember
who I am

and you make me
feel soft

in a hard world.

Like a feather
falling from a skyscraper.

Like the last star
in a universe

filled with darkness.

You have saved me.
You have made me realize

how much life
I have left.

You've kept me
where I belong.

EVERYWHERE YOU GO

All that you need
you carry

with you—you take
 with you.

So if it is
a person

that you need.

Then let it be known
that when you

depart
you take

a piece of their heart
in your hands.

In your soul.

In your thoughts
 and memories.

You take them with you
and have the gift

to love them...
everywhere you go.

Never take that
for granted.

A LITTLE HARDER

You just don't.

You fight for them
no matter how hard

it gets.

You fight with them
no matter what

ends up
happening.

No matter what
the outcome is.

You don't give up
on the people you love.

You just don't.

Doing so
will be something

that will eat you
alive

and you will never

forgive yourself
for not trying

a little harder.

You will always
wonder why

and what if.

And it will always
come back to haunt you

no matter who
you end up with.

No matter where you go.

No matter who you meet
and who you don't.

You don't give up
on the people

you love.

Period.

You just don't.

You give it your all

until there's nothing left
of you.

Until it kills you.

It is better to die

trying

than to live

knowing

you could have
loved

a little harder.

SAD PART

The sad part was,

I spent most of my life
looking for a love

I knew
never existed.

Chasing people
 I knew

I didn't deserve.

And writing poetry
that didn't really matter

to anyone
but myself.

After all this time
the world is still

a very,
very

lonely place.

WISH IT

As long
as you wish it...

always know
that you can

start over.

That you can
pick yourself up

right where
you began

to fall apart.

That there's always
a new day tomorrow

and that you can
always choose

to love yourself
and chase

what you deserve
when you need it most.

As long as you

wish it.

As long as you know
what you deserve.

SOMEONE

Don't let them
turn you

into someone
you can't recognize.

Into someone
cold and cruel.

Into someone
who doesn't care

or love.

Don't let them
change you

or hurt you.

Don't let them
make you believe

that you are incapable
of love.

That you are
not worthy

or deserving of it.

You are so much more
and they are too.

It is just,
sometimes

we don't know
what we are capable of.

Sometimes
we don't know

who we are
or what we're supposed

to do.

Who
we're supposed

to love
and who

we're supposed
to let go.

But still,
don't let them change you.

Don't let them break you
or turn you

into someone else.

Believe
in what you have
within.

Hold it.

Harness it
for what it is—for

the light it radiates.

Your soul
is a star

and your heart
is a goddamn galaxy

waiting to be discovered.

And some people
are astronomers,

scientist of the heavens
and some are gazers

waiting to reach

the stars
but have no way
of going.

It is true.

Some chase the light
and some become it...

and then
there's you.

And you know
what exists

inside of you.

So keep shining.

Keep glowing
through the darkness.

It is
what it is

and you
just have to learn

not to change
for no one.

And if you do,
make sure

it's for the best.

That's all.

FREE YOURSELF

You don't have to
impress anyone

and you don't
have to

be nice
or polite

either.

You just have
to be yourself

even if it makes
them uncomfortable.

Be yourself
even if

the outcome hurts.

Not everyone
is going to like you

or be there
for you.

So why
do you feel obligated

to try
to be friends

with people
who don't

genuinely care
about you.

Why
do you feel

compelled
to apologize

for things
that are not

your fault.

You don't have to
do

none of these
things.

You just
keep your head up,

smile
and keep it moving.

I know this is cliché

But goddamnit!

Your world
should revolve

around you
and your happiness

and nothing else.

AMEN.

DON'T SEE IT COMING

You shouldn't
have to force

someone
to love you.

Let it come
naturally.

Sometimes
the best relationships

in life...

are the ones
we don't see

coming.

*The few we don't
expect.*

MORE HOPE

We have this
tendency

to ignore
the ignored.

This tendency
to forget our past—to

forget
how to attend

to ourselves.

We forget
so many things

and it's not because
of this

or that.

It's because
we are all

so caught up
in the present

that

we barely give
any thought

to our past—to
our future.

Everything is sadness.
Everything is stress.

Everything is debt.

Everything in the *now*
is shoved down our throats

to the point
that we can't

make room for anything
that matters.

For things
we once looked forward to

or spent
our time on.

We have forgotten
how to live,

what to live for
and why.

We have forgotten
what's important to us.

We have forgotten
the well-being

of other people.

It's hard to see
others empowering others.

It's hard to see
others wanting others

to succeed.

It's rare to see people
really care.

Really feel things
with their souls

and change.

We have so much
to look forward to

but it is hard

to indulge in these things
when everything

I need
to survive

keeps bringing me down...
keeps

blinding me
to what's really

in my heart.

We need less pain.

Less suffering.
Less stress.

Less debt.
Less agony.

Less systematic platforms
designed to bring us down.

We need less war
and more love.

More friendship—comradeship.

We need more understanding.

More hope.
More respect.

More rest.
More humanity...

but it's brutal out there,

that
I know

and it's hard
to abide by these things.

It's hard
to follow your childhood

dreams—to
remember

what your life was
before the responsibilities.

But this,
I urge of you.

This
I want for you,

all of you.

Find victory
in tragedy.

Find light
in darkness.

Find laughter
in tears.

Find joy
in stress.

And find love
in hatred.

Everything is connected.
Everything is balanced.

You just have to
pay attention

and stop ignoring
the solutions when they

are presented
to you

right before your eyes.

So it may be
a good thing

or even a bad thing.

But it is up to you
to find the goodness

in all things.

It is up to you
to not let things

terrible things
that press you down

affect you.

Life can be beautiful
but only

if you let it be.

And only
if you pay attention

to all the things
you deserve.

MAYBE LOVE

Maybe love
isn't what we've been

told.

Maybe it's not
all romance

and not
all attraction.

Maybe love is a friend.

Someone
who understands you.

Someone
who wants what's best

for you
and prays for you

especially
when you're at

your worst.

WHAT WE WANT

All of my life
I've been told

to wait.

To be patient.

To just
let things happen

on their own.

All of my life
I've been led

to believe,
that if

it's meant
for me

then I shouldn't
have to

worry
about anything.

That

if it's written...
it will occur.

That

it will come
to me.

And in all my years,
I've been waiting...

in all my years,
I've let

so many things
pass me by.

I've lost too much
and I've gained...

too little.

I've given my soul
and I've received

barely anything
back

in return.

So I don't

want to believe
that if it's meant

to happen,
then

I should just
let things be

on their own.

Let things
come to me

at their own
pace.

No.
fucks that.

If I have a dream
I want to work on it.

I want to
believe in it.

Envision it
for my own.

I want to build
on it.

Day by day.
Hour by hour.

Until one day,
I wake up,

look back
and see

all the progress
I've made.

I want to believe
in myself

and not just
destiny.

I want to trust
what I'm capable of.

Trust
what I know

can be done.

And it's the same thing
with you.

I don't want to
wait around anymore.

I don't want to
watch you slip

through my hands.

I want to work on *us*.

Day by day.
Hour by hour.

I want to feed
your heart

and water
your soul.

I want to let
things be

but only because
we let it be.

Because

we want it
to be.

Let me be your sun.
Your moon.

Your planet.

Let me be
the lover you need.

Let me follow you.
Grow with you.

Heal with you.

To fill the cracks
and the void.

Let me love you
and let me do it now...

unconditionally
and without

regret.

I don't want to waste
my time

waiting around for you
to be mine.

I don't want to sit around
and wonder.

Let us sit
on the sun

with all reason,
and let us create

a place

where all the things
we want to happen...

happen

but only
because we want them

to
and only

because we put the effort
in all the things

we want
to stay.

FEEL ME NOW

Feel me.

I have more soul
than you think.

More pain.
More laughter.

More tears.
More love.

Feel me.

From the moment
you met me,

to the moment
we said good-bye.

I have always
had more.

I have always
felt more...

but I have also,
shared less.

Said less
and the moment

you met me,
I loved you.

I had it
in for you.

For us.

For what
we could have been.

But instead,
I let myself drown.

I let myself
drift away.

I let myself
hurt you,

the only person
I could trust.

Goddamn
it's a fucking shame.

It really is.
And I still

don't understand
why I did

what I did
to you.

I still don't understand
why I push

people away.

Why I have this
tendency

to distance myself
from the people

I love
or why

I have this
terrible habit

to detach myself
from anything

and anyone
who gets too close.

Maybe I'm afraid
of loss.

Maybe I'm afraid
of getting hurt first.

Of being broken
by someone

I thought
who'd always be there

for me.

It's ironic,
I know.

I break the people
I love.

I leave the people
whom I want

to stay.

Just feel me
on this one.

Just try to understand.

It's me.
It's not you.

It's really me.

The thing is,
I don't know what

to do
with all of this love

I have trapped
within me.

And I don't know
how

to let it out
properly…

but it does
have a hold of me.

And I wish
I could have shared it

with you.

But instead,
I let you go

without reason
and let you go...

with regret
and I'm sorry

for that.

Someway,
somehow,

for me,

my story
always ends

with being alone…
but that is something

I have to live
with on my own.

It is my own burden.

My own curse.

NOTHING IS HERE

Sometimes
you just have to let go.

No matter how much
love you have for them.

Sometimes
you have to find the courage
within you

to move on,
to start over,

and to *hope*
for nothing

but the best
from here on out.

NOT FOR ANY ONE

You don't feel the need
to change when everyone else
is changing.

You don't go through seasons,
through these phases,

although,
you hold the moon
in your hands

and the sun
in your heart.

You stay true
to your feelings.

You stay true
to who you are—to who
you want to become.

You take care
of your well-being,

of your soul,
when the chaos surrounds you.

You know the difference

between
what hurts
and what doesn't

and bravely enough,
you feel them both
at the same time.

You're strong
and I don't just say that

to build your confidence.

I don't just say that
to give you hope.

I say that
because you're exhausted.

We all are.

I say that
because you still have a fight
in you.

This beautiful way
of undoing yourself.

This beautiful way
of collecting who you are.

Especially
under these rough conditions.

You fall apart in such a way
that I could only admire you

as it happens.

You're an angel
searching for her wings.

A bird
searching for the perfect sky.

A dream
searching for the perfect person
to inspire.

And you'll never stop searching,

not until you find it.

You're willing to go through hell
and back

for what you believe in
and you won't change

for anyone.

You stay true

to yourself

no matter how tragic things get.

You go out
and spread love

as long as you have
the heart for it.

You shed tears,
keep your head up high,
and keep it moving...

and that's what makes you

so goddamn beautiful.

SOME YEARS

A friend of mine lost his job.

He gave them 19 years,
can you believe that?

19 whole years
of sweat and blood
and maybe even

tears.

He said he doesn't know
what to do.

He doesn't know
where to pick up again.

Doesn't know
who he now is,

as he has been doing this
for so long

that it was a part of himself.

I told him that life goes on.
That people move on.
That what you once knew

will come back
around again.

People change.
Lovers leave.
Jobs get replaced.
Hearts break.
Children grow.
Wars continue.

And laughter still
floods the street.

19 years.

And sometimes in life
that's how it happens.

You give someone 19 years
of your life.

Of your heart.
Of your soul.

And in an instant
it disappears.

What you once knew
is over

and you are left

with no options

other than
to move on.

FADE AWAY

It hurts
when they slowly
fade away.

When they slowly
lose interest in you.

When they slowly
move on

without telling you
why.

It hurts.

To live with a heart
full of worry

and act
as if it doesn't affect you—

to watch them
severe your veins...

while pretending
it doesn't hurt

at all.

THE FIRST PERSON

The first person
who breaks your heart

will always teach you
the importance of love.

1. People come and go
and only a handful of them

are willing to stay.

So it is best
to give them your promises.

2. You have to go through pain
every once in a while.

That's how it works.

Pain is inevitable.
Pain is relative.

Pain brings people
closer together.

So it is best to give the people
you love your sorrow.

They will make flowers
out of them.

Believe it.

And

3. Somewhere down the line
a revelation will hit you

like a comet
and when it does

you will think of the first time
you got your heart broken.

And the second
and maybe even the third.

And you will finally realize
the importance of it all.

And you will thank them
for the experiences.

And you will finally bring down
your walls

and learn how to move on.

How to forgive.

How to properly heal.

And you will do
all of these marvelous things

but also,
you will never forget the way
they once made you feel.

You will never forget
the slow burn

that

brokenness brings.

And you will
remind yourself of it

every now and then...
and you will do so

to remember
the importance of letting go
and etc.

To remember
why you should never search
for love in the same place
you lost it.

Why you should never
search for love

in the same place
where it left you broken.

That's the importance of love.

Of going through it—to have it
and cherish it...

but also,
to not fall victim

to the same people
and tragedies that made you feel
even more alone.

To not fall victim
to all things

that covered up the sun.

Those lessons are valuable,
therefore,

it is best to learn
as much as you can

and love
as much as you're willing

to get hurt.

Stay strong.

FURTHER AWAY

I don't know
how to give you

want you need
without losing

a part of myself

I know
I will deeply regret.

And I still don't know
how to love you

without

pushing you further away
a little more.

AFTER TOMORROW

In the end,
we always have

something to lose.

Something we regret.

That's life.

We anticipate so much.

Some that happen

and some
that never reach the shore.

That never reach us
when we need them most.

And for what?
To live for a moment?

To believe in something
or have something

to keep you going.

It is all for a reason.

All for hope
and love.

For something,
anything,
to hold on to.

To take with you
as time goes on.

I have learned,
in all my years,

that

in the end,
that is what we live for.

The little moments.
The little victories.

Whether we keep them
or not.

LESSONS

The best lesson
you can ever give someone

is

the realization
of self-love.

And that alone
is the most

valuable lesson
in the world.

I AM NOT SCARED

You do not
terrify me.

You give me strength.

And I'm asking you
to love me

when I am falling apart.

When I have nothing left
to give.

And when I am broken down
to the smallest parts of myself.

That is all.
Nothing major.

To love me
and leave nothing

behind.

To love me
and

celebrate what we have

until our bones
are the only thing

left.

IF THEY

If they love you,

they'll make the effort.

They'll be there for you
when you need them most.

They'll try to understand you
even when they don't see

eye to eye with you.

They'll support you
no matter what—in anything
you wish to chase.

They'll correct you
when you're wrong.

Teach you
when you need guidance.

Lead you
when you feel lost

and let you move on

when you're ready

to be on your own.

If they love you,
they'll set you free,

but never quite
stop looking out for you.

No matter what happens.
No matter how far you go.

Lovers come in
and out of our lives

but true friendship
is hard to come by.

Hard to forget.

And

even harder
to let go.

Remember this.

THE POSIBILITY

Everything and anything
is possible

when you open your heart.

When you
open yourself

to everything that hurts.

This is where
you will unlock

what truly matters.

Where you will find
the kind of love

that will keep your heart
young forever.

That will keep your
soul on fire.

DESERVE

We deserve
some kind of love.

Soft and gentle.
Fun and sad.

But never haunting
when it leaves.

We all deserve
some kind of love.

As long as we are ready
to let it go.

As long as we know
nothing is forever.

Everything has its place.

Its rightful moment
to exist

and disappear.

From you
to me.

The clock is
always ticking.

NOTHING LEFT

There is nothing left
for you to hurt.

Nothing left
to bury.

Or kill.
Or label.
Or misconstrue.

My world has ended
many times before.

But it has also
begun.

I am endless.

And everyday
I am different.

And you can try
to hold me back.

Break me down.
Destroy me

or hate me.

But like the shoreline,

I will always come back.

Always return stronger
and kinder.

Tougher
and softer.

This is the way I heal.

The way I live
and survive.

This is the way I love.

And there is
nothing you can do

to change that.

LOVE MORE PLEASE

Love more.
Let it be religion.

Give in to it.

Let it defeat you
but not destroy you.

Let it define you
but not control you.

Let it fill you
but not empty you.

Love more.
Doubt less.

Love more.
Fear less.

Feel more.
Criticize less—hate less.

Stand for something.
Fall for nothing.

Let it be religion.

Praise what you
hold within.

Then release it
to the world.

There is so much
to live for.

So much to do
and abide for.

Don't ever lose
sight of this:

There are so many
reasons to die for.

Let love
be one of them.

SAY A WORD

We didn't have
to say a word.

We didn't have
to do

all of those things

we thought
we had to do

for each other
to show each other

we cared.

That we loved.

That we wanted to be
a part of each other's lives.

We didn't do
any of that.

We just knew.

And it was
the kind of knowing

we didn't have
to reassure.

We didn't have
to prove.

We just knew.

From the moment we met.

We knew.

It was
that kind of love.

That kind
of connection

and it was

the kind
that moved

the soul.

STORIES

You tell stories
that only

I can relate to.

That only
I can feel.

This is why I love you.

I see myself in you.
I feel a piece

of what I love

bloom

out of your soul.

NO EARS HERE

You stop apologizing
for yourself

the moment you realize
what you feel.

What you know.
What you are.

And that

YOU ARE

of your own creation

and not
of the work of others.

Not the work
of anyone

but yourself.

You are responsible
for what

you put out.

What you put
into your soul.

No one
owes you anything.

And you don't
owea damn thing

to anyone.

Your life
is your life.

Stop apologizing
for what you are.

Become
who you want

to become.

Offend
who you want

to offend
while doing so.

The world
doesn't give you mercy

and neither should you.

Be fierce.
Be strong.
Be unapologetic.

Find your place.

Accept
and love yourself

for who you are.

It is more terrifying
to be

and do less.

It is a waste
to try and

go against yourself.

To make yourself

believe
you are a wave,

when indeed,

you are

very much
like an ocean.

Stay Beautiful,
my friends.

IF YOU

If you haven't
been yourself lately.

If you've ever
felt lost

or empty

and

cannot explain why.

If you've been looking
for something

you don't even know
exists.

If you've been asking questions,
perhaps even

the wrong ones,
and still

have yet
to receive an answer.

If you don't know

who you are.

If you don't know
why you're here.

If you don't know
why you feel

the way you feel.

And lastly,
if you feel more alone

than the night before.

I understand you.

I feel what you feel.

I've asked the same questions
and I've wondered

all my life
about
the same things,
too.

I have my own demons
and I'm still struggling

with them

every day.

This is my truth.

This is my soul...
and I hope

my horrors leave you
with something.

I hope
they give you

the strength you
need to carry on.

The courage you need
to move on,

to let go
of whatever hurts you.

There still hope...
there always is,

no matter how far
in you are.

The light,
that little spark

of hope,

will always
show you the way.

SOME PEOPLE

Some people
never give up

on the people
they love.

And some will call it
a curse—a burden

of pain
and suffering,

but I call it

struggling
and fighting

for someone worth it—for
something you know

you deserve.

DO NOT LET...

Don't let your heart
lose hope.

The wrong people
will exit your life

when they have to
and the right ones

will find you
when you need them most.

Trust the process.

Find comfort
in your timing

and let time decide
who gets to stay.

Worry less
and trust the process

a little more.

OF YOURSELF

You have to take care
of yourself entirely.

Not just your heart
but your mind,

soul and body.

You have to protect
yourself at all costs

but not just from relationships
and getting your heart broken

but from external factors
that are meant to bring you down.

Protect your mind
and your thoughts.

Protect your body
from processed foods.

Protect your soul
from bad energies

and focus
on what matters

to you.

Focus
on what you love.

Focus
on spreading love.

Focus on healing.

So many of us
are wanting to heal.

And so many of us
don't know how

or where to start.

Just focus on yourself.
Take time on yourself.

It all begins
with you.

That's all.

LEARN THIS

You have to learn
how to accept yourself

for who you are.

Be comfortable
in your own skin,
you know?

You have to embrace it,
make the best of it.

And if you're not happy,
then you have the right

to take time
on yourself,

to work on yourself.

But you have to be patient.

It's not going to happen
overnight

and it's not
something

someone else
could do for you either.

You are what you are
and what you want

to change
is something

only you can do
for yourself.

Just remember
to stay beautiful, baby,

and remember
to always chase

the things
you deserve..

CONVERSATIONS

Sometimes
having a conversation

in a parked car
for hours

can heal you
in ways you never thought
possible.

It can be therapeutic.

It can sometimes save you
from yourself.

AFRAID OF US

They want us
to be ourselves

but only
if it's within their terms.

They want us
to be free

but as long
as we don't go
far enough.

And then
they ask us

why are we so mad.

They ask us
why are we so bitter

towards the future
and so hateful

towards the past.

So much
that they become

afraid of us
in the present.

So much
that they use the media

to dumb us down—to
calm us down.

To lie to us
and hide the truth.

The problem isn't us.
The problem is them...

the older generation
who closed our future.

The older generation
who wanted peace

but failed to grant it
with love.

No.

Instead they brought war.

They brought death
and blood
and pain

and suffering
to the future generations.

Then they wonder
why we are so *goddamn mad.*

You killed everything
we stand for.

Everything that's beautiful.

Everything that gives light
and life

and it all was done
to make money.

Something you also
created

to oppress us.

Something you created
to manufacture

this fake happiness
we have

for yourselves.

DO NOT RUN

You shouldn't run back
to those who broke you.

To those
who've left you

in the dark.

You can't grow a flower
without the use of light.

Sometimes
You have to grow a garden
in the middle of a desert.

Let that sink in.

You beautiful, motherfucker.

A LITTLE PAIN

You don't realize
how much you deserve,

not until
you've been through hell

with someone.

The same way
you don't appreciate love

without going
through a little

pain.

I CARE

And you pretend
you don't care.

And you act
like it doesn't bother you.

And you want to forget
but all you do is remember.

And it hurts even more
when you're alone.

And everyone is laughing
but deep down inside you're sad.

And you try to move on
but can't.

And you want to let go
but some things

are just too damn hard
to get rid of.

And you cry
when no one is around.

And you want to be happy

but you find it difficult
to laugh again.

And you try so hard
to fill the void with other people.

And sometimes those same people
make you feel more alone.

And you're lost
without the one you left behind.

And you just want to be found.
(Anywhere but here)

And you just want
to put everything behind you.

And you've tried almost everything
and nothing has worked.

And this is how you live your life.

This is how it hurts.

This is how the stars die,
but also,

how they are born.

This is how you take it all in.

The pain fills
and the sorrow follows

and the memories can't seem
to fade.

It hurts… as it always does
and as it should.

Sometimes you just can't
get it together

without the people
you love.

WHAT IS IT

What is it that you're avoiding?
Is it love?
Is it friendship?

I know you're exhausted.
I can see it in your eyes.

I know you've been through hell.

I know your heart is worn
and beaten.

I know.

You don't have to say a word.

I sense it.

I can feel what hurts.
I can relate to your pain.

To your tragedy.

You're sad,
of course you are...

Because you think
your life isn't going as planned.

Because almost everything
you do

leads you toward some kind
of terrible disappointment—

toward the wrong kind
of people to love.

It's hard.

All of it is.

From what you feel
to how you want to express yourself

and execute your heart
to the world.

It's hard
and letting others know
who you are is hard,

too hard.

I know,
but please...

Don't close your heart.

Don't walk away
from the possibility
and please don't stop believing.

Hope is a beautiful thing.

A miraculous thing
and everything you're going through
I feel as well.

Because you're not alone,
you never were

and you never will be.

So stop telling yourself
that you are.

Stop letting your mind
play tricks on you

and stop trying to convince yourself
that you are not capable
of love.

That you're not capable
of more—of what you deserve.

You're beautiful,
baby,

don't let your doubts destroy
who you really are.

Keep shining.

SOME, NOT ALL

Some good-byes
are easy
and then there are some
that are hard.

No one ever likes
letting people go.

No one ever likes
being the one
who cuts the line.

But what is right is right.

And you can't be with someone
if they love someone else.

You can't be with someone
because they're bored

or because
they're using you
to pass their time.

You can't.

That's not right.
That's not fair.

Find someone
who loves you
genuinely.

Find someone
who has grown from their past,

not someone who is *still*
living in it.

Find someone,
anyone, who'll make you
a better person.

That's the goal.

That's the reason we search

for certain people—for someone

to love…
and to hold.

HAVE NOT LEARNED

If life has taught us anything,
then it has taught us

that finding someone
you connect with

is just as rare
and as beautiful

as losing someone
you once loved

or cared about.

Life teaches us many things
but finding balance in receiving

and letting go
is just as important…

as finding balance
in happiness and sadness—in love

and pain.

Balance is key.

And sometimes you're going to win...

while other times

you're going to sit back
and cry.

And it's the same with people.

You lose one to gain another
and somewhere in-between
you must find peace.

You must accept the way
they come and go…

and understand

how they come to you
when you need them the most
and vice versa.

Life,
like people,

change

but the trick is
to remember those

who are worth remembering

and find balance

in all things

that are meant
to make you fall.

That are meant
to make you feel...

free.

LESS ALONE PT 3

You make me feel less alone
and I don't mean a time

or a place
or being together,

somewhere on the edge
of the world.

I mean,
when I'm alone in my bed.

Alone in the middle of the street.

Alone somewhere,
anywhere, on the planet.

When I close my eyes
or when I wake…

you make me *feel less alone.*

Because we're lovers,
you and I,

we look at the details
and let our hearts lead the way.

So whether we're together in a room
or cities apart,

or even countries,

I look up toward the moon
and feel secure.

And I do so
because

I know you're out there,
breathing...

surviving...

thinking and feeling
the same way as me.

And because of that...
I feel less alone.

I feel like you.

Like you and I are the last people
on the planet...

and we have our entire lives
to convince each other

and ourselves
of why we are capable of love—
of so much more.

We deserve it,

you and I,

we deserve people
who make us feel

less alone.

People who bring out
the best parts of eachother.

People who make us feel

like we are

in love
with ourselves.

YOU DON'T KNOW

You don't know
how hard it is

for me
to be myself.

For me to speak my mind
in a place

that keeps telling me
what to feel.

In a world that keeps
shoving me
with what to think.

So I say it like this

because

it is the only way
I know how.

These are my feelings:
black and white.

These are my scars:
hot and cold.

And you can either
accept them
or leave them.

Love them
or misunderstand them

for what they are.

This is what I do
and this is what I've done

and these are my
contradictions.

My flesh
is of my flesh

and my blood
is of my blood.

And I don't need
some asshole in the media

to tell me the difference
between the two.

Thisis my heart.
This is my mind.

And what connects the two

is a bridge
that only I can cross.

That only I can build
if it falls.

This is what hurts.
This is how my heart falls

and this is how
I heal the two,

bond the two.

And I will live
the way I must,

although,
the world will continue
to bring me pain.

Let me be
who I want to be

and let my mind travel
the undiscovered road
that waits ahead.

Let me allow
who I want
in my life.

And let me love freely
without conviction.

This is all I ask of you.
Is it too much?

You already have control
of everything else.

Let me have
a piece of myself back.

That is all I ask.

Let me love
who I want to love.

And let me do so
freely.

Give me a piece
of the world

and I will return it
back to you

better than it was
before.

IN SAND

It's not you.

It's just
you keep giving your heart

to the wrong
type of people.

People who haven't grown
or matured.

People who haven't
been through enough.

Who haven't been hurt
enough

to understand what it's like
to drown in sand—

what it's like to drown
in an ocean of fire.

So it's not you,
although,

they'll make you *think* it is
but it's not.

Believe me it's not.

It's just some people
have a way of pulling your heart.

Some people
have a way

of bringing out
different sides of you.

Both beautiful and ugly.

So it's definitely not your fault
for feeling too deeply.

For giving chances
and letting things in

the way you do.

And it's not your fault
for not knowing

what's good for you either.

Because it's hard
figuring things out like that.

It's hard
knowing what you deserve

and don't.

It's hard
choosing between

what's right for you
and what hurts,

no matter how much love
you have for those

who've done you wrong.

It's hard
and it takes time,

and there's no easy way to put it
without making you feel

some sort of way

but you have to *move on.*

You have to come
to the realization that some people

aren't meant
to be yours—no matter how much

history you have together
and no matter how much

time you've put into them.

You have to let go sometimes
and understand

that maybe it's not you
because you've done

all that you can.

That maybe it's them
and that maybe

starting over

can be the change you need

to move on...
after all.

GO SILENT

Don't tell them it's okay
when you know it's not.

Don't let your feelings fade
into the darkness.

Don't let your voice go silent.

Let them know
what's in your heart.

Let them know
how beautiful it is

to be understood.

How beautiful it is
to have someone you can trust—

to speak to
about anything.

Be open.

Share what's on your mind.

And never go quietly
into the dark.

People will always
appreciate you for your honesty,

and love you
for what you carry within your heart.

So speak up,
tell it how it is.

If it hurts,
then it hurts.

I just want to make sure
you're not censoring yourself.

You deserve so much more
than that,

and believe...

that the reassurance of self

is more valuable
than anything else.

EXCEPT HOPE

It is my will
to choose someone

who supports my appetite
for life.

Someone
who compels my voice.

Who strengthens my vision.

It is my will
to be with someone

who understands me.

Who makes me feel
real.

Someone who isn't afraid
to explore the soul—

the deeper meaning
of pain and love.

It is my will
to feed off their fire.

To live by it.

To exchange it
when needed most.

And to comfort each other
when things seem

to be falling apart.

It is my will,
and mine only...

and it should be yours
as well.

Life is too short
to not live it

any other way.

To not to chase
what you desire

or what you know
you deserve.

Life is too fragile
to *NOT* seek others

who seek the same things

and others who are looking
for another way out.

Another way to love.

To die.
To live.

To forgive and heal.

Find them,
for they are out there

and find them
because they are out

looking for you.

It is your will
and nothing is ever determined

except for hope.

Hope you find them

and

hope they are everything
you need

and more.

HOMES

You were built
for this.

To search for those
who were meant

to make a home
of your heart.

To search for those
who were meant
to make you feel.

But always remember

you do NOT belong to them.

You belong to yourself
and if you wish to share

yourself

is completely up to you.

No one owns you.
No one can dictate

what you feel or whom

you are.

I hope you understand this.
You are meant to be free.

Meant to share
what you love

with others
but never meant

to be caged in.

TWO PEOPLE

Two people
opening their hearts

at the right moment
and at the right time

is not
a coincidence.

It's a goddamn miracle.

EXACTLY WHAT IT IS

You're exactly
where you need to be.

So don't go ahead
and start looking

for shortcuts.

Don't go ahead
and start wanting

to skip through things
that are meant for you.

The best kind of people
live through

what they're meant for
and learn from it.

They go through life
taking it all in

and at their own pace
too.

From people.
To moments.

To places.

Never rush
what's waiting for you.

And never take
anything for granted.

From good times
to bad.

It is all for something.
It always is.

OUT ALIVE

*Your scars
are more than just scars.*

*They represent
how strong you are.*

*The times you thought
it was the end*

*but made it out
alive.*

CHIME IN

What is sad
is how everyone tells you

how one day
you'll find

someone perfect for you.

To be patient
with the love you have

and just wait
for that perfect person

to chime in.

But what they fail
to say is,

to practice
being alone.

To give the love
you have within

to yourself.

To not just wait

and sit around
for someone to make you happy.

That all
that happiness

you harbor
can be unlocked

for yourself.

So yes,

they tell you
that your one true love

is out there.

There is no doubt in that
but what they forget

to mention is,
how the love you have

within
is initially

meant for you.

You just have the privilege
to share it

with someone you care about.

That's all.

STARTING OVER

It's a lot
having to start over

with someone new.

The thought of it
can be exhausting.

But I will tell you this.

If it's meant for you
it will be.

And it will be easy.
It will be effortless.

And believe me,
it will be *beautiful*.

YOU DON'T KNOW

You don't know
emptiness

until you've kissed
someone

who is no longer
in love with you.

DAMN.

YOU DON'T KNOW II

You don't know
what you're made of

until

you're forced
to let go

of someone
you love.

DAMN.

PERIOD

No love
is the wrong kind
of love.

It is just
some people have

a different way
of giving it.

And a different way
of receiving it.

It's all about
your expectations of it.

What you know
you deserve.

If they show you otherwise.
Then it is not love.

Period.

DESTROY YOU

You're not the one
who has broken

me down.

I have done this
to myself.

I have allowed you
to have some sort

of say
in what I do.

And because of that
it has affected the way

I feel.

But it is not you.
You don't have

that kind of power
over me.

That kind of say.

It only happens

if I allow it to
and sometimes,

foolishly,
it ends up like this.

So don't apologize
for something you have no

control over.

Don't think
for one second

you caused
all of this pain in me.

I care too much
and I love the same way

my mother once did.

I cannot help it.
It runs through my blood.

I love you
but you did not hurt me.

I did this
to myself

and because of it,
now I must go.

I must wander off
and find myself again.

Because that, too,
is something

only I can do myself.
Only I

can learn
how to rebuild

something
I let get destroyed.

VALIDATION

You have nothing
to prove to anyone.

You know
who you are.

You know
how you feel.

What you've been through.
What you've had

to let go of
in order to be

who you are.

You don't need
the validation

of others
only of yourself.

Seek
what you seek within.

Find
what you find within.

It is all there.

It is all revealed
with time.

JUST WAIT.
AND WAIT AND WAIT.

IT IS NEVER THE END.
ALWAYS

THE BEGINNING.

FEEL SAD

I don't know why
the most broken

smile the hardest.

I don't know why
they laugh

when all they really feel
is

sadness.

SAVE YOUR ENERGY

Don't forget
that you are someone too

and that no one
can take your place.

So just because
you love them

doesn't give them
the right to take you

for granted.

Don't allow them
to take advantage of you.

Don't allow them
to disrespect you.

To tell you
you're replaceable.

To tell you
all sorts of things

that break your self-esteem
and make you feel guilty

for the way
you love.

For the way you feel.

You are someone too.
And you should be treated

the way
you treat them.

So raise
your middle finger up high

and fuck them
for giving you

anxiety
and not love.

Fuck them
for causing you

depression
and not granting you comfort.

And *fuck* them
for filling your soul

with emptiness
and not filling

it with gentleness.

You're beautiful, baby
and you don't need that type

of negativity
in your life.

You don't need
that type of energy.

You are more valuable
than you think.

WHY THEY LEAVE

"It hurts
when people leave."

"Of course it does.
Because it's like

losing a part of yourself
you finally learned

 to love.

Like finding it one day
and losing it

the next.

Forever."

CHANCE TO MEET

People want to love.

They want to remember it.
Hold on to it.

Be in-between it.

No one ever
really wants to be

alone.

There's no beauty in that.

No life.
No breath.
No growth.

There's nothing poetic
about being alone.

Just regret and a life

full of people
you wish

you had the chance
to meet.

SOME PEOPLE

Some People
are like birds.

Some fly out
of cages.

While others
choose to stay

in them
forever.

A GIRL

A girl writes to me
on *Facebook*.

The message said.

*"I hope one day
I can write*

as good as you."

My love.
My dear.

My sweet human.

It is not
about the words

that flow out of me.

It is about the feelings.
The many years of pain.

The many years of tears.
Of feeling abandoned.

Of feeling empty.
Of feeling

like I am *not* worth a damn.

My love.
My dear.

My sweet human.

It has nothing to do
with talent or skill.

Nothing to do
with that.

It is about
what I've been through.

The years
and years

and years
of trying to find myself.

And the many horrors
it took

to get to
where I am.

Find yourself
through the fire.

Find yourself
through your pain.

Be you.
Be who you feel.

Write like you.

Write what hurts.

FUCK AWAY

The truth is,
I don't know

what kind of love
I want

but I do know
I don't want

the kind of love
I've already had.

The kind of love
that has left me broken.

With more questions
than answers.

With more pain
than love.

More emptiness.
Numbness.

I don't know
who I want

or when or even where

but I do know
I don't want

what I've experienced.

I don't need
that type of shit

in my life.

I don't want it.

**Please
stay the fuck**

away.

SOMETHING YOU LOVE

Absence
can either work

with you
or against you.

It can make people
miss you

or forget you.

Need you
or move away from you.

Absence
is a delicate little thing.

And it shouldn't be
taken too lightly.

You might lose
something you love.

BREATHE AGAIN

Your love
is not for everyone.

It is for you.

Love yourself
until there is nothing left

but bones
and sand.

Love yourself
and keep a piece of it safe.

Throw it in the ocean.

Lose it.
Hide it.

But find it
when you need

to breathe.

PEOPLE PASS

People die
from having a broken heart.

So it is best
to give it to someone

who knows
how to protect it.

Who knows how
not to let it slip away.

Someone like you
who knows how serious

letting a human heart fall
can be.

People die
from having a broken heart.

All the time.

It's just not on the news.
Not on the paper.

Not on social media.
It's not something

we talk about.

Not something
we take too seriously.

People die
from having a broken heart.

They fall within.
They get lost somewhere

in the darkness
of themselves.

Somewhere
in the chaos of it all.

People die
from having a broken heart.

They die silently.
They die

after not knowing
how to ask for help.

After not knowing
who to run to.

Who to pour themselves to.
They die alone

from being afraid

of
being alone.

They let the sadness
consume them.

Consume whatever it is
they have left.

People do die
from this.

They really do.

And it's one
of the saddest things

in the world.

So it shouldn't be taken
too lightly.

And you shouldn't
just give your heart

to anyone.

It's *that* fragile.
It's *that* soft.

That easy to lose.
Easy to watch slip away.

People do die
from a broken heart.

And almost everyone thinks
it won't happen to them.

That the person
they give their heart to

will never do
such a thing.

We are that naive.
That loving.

That caring.
That trustworthy.

We want to believe
in people.

We want to believe
that they can possibly

do us
no harm.

That they are not capable

of such things.

We really want to give ourselves
to the people we want to love.

But it's not like that.

Sadly
some people are *really* undeserving.

Some people
have no idea

what to do with the love
of others.

Let alone their own.

Some people are so cruel.
Are so hurt

and so lost—that
they think everyone is out

to get them.

Therefore,
it is in their nature

to destroy.
To dismantle

before they get themselves hurt.

Some people
have it all backwards.

They do more harm
than good.

They take more
then they receive.

They devour
and devour and devour

the souls of others.

So yes.
It is true.

People die from having
a broken heart.

It is no laughing matter.
But some people die

before
without even realizing it.

They take the love
of others
and starve it.

And that,
my sweet friends,

is worse
than death itself.

People die
from having a broken heart.

But nothing
is as bad

as breaking the people
who actually care.

Nothing is as bad
as causing it.

As giving doom to someone
who wants to love you.

That's a terrible gift to give.

A terrible curse
to runaway from.

And a terrible way
to kill someone

you love.

BRAVE ENOUGH

She said
she wasn't ready.

Wasn't ready
to move on.

To leave behind
what we had built

for several years.

She said
she wasn't ready

for the world.

One without me.
One without *us*.

I didn't know
what to do.

I didn't know
what I wanted.

We had been so fucked up lately
that we no longer had

respect for one another.

I would hurt her
and she would hurt me.

And sometimes
I think we did it on purpose.

Sometimes
I think we did it to each other

because of what
the other had done

days before.

And we both knew
it was wrong.

We both knew
we'd come back, too.

One way or another
no matter who caused what.

We always seemed
to find a way back.

An excuse, you know?

And I think we did it

because none of us
had the courage to leave.

The courage
to *really* move on.

To start over
with someone new.

Someone we would have
to take a risk on.

Maybe it was love.
Or maybe it wasn't.

I don't know.

But what I do know is,
we had more bad memories

than good.

More times breaking up—making
up, than enjoying

what we had.

It's a hard position to be in.
To know exactly

what you deserve

and still
put up with the bullshit

you're given.

To know exactly
what you have to do

but not be brave enough
to go through with it.

It's a hard decision to do.
Because although

I knew what I needed.

What I deserved.
Something inside of me

was telling me
I wasn't ready too.

Something inside of me
was telling me

I couldn't possibly move on.
Not from this.

Not from her.
It's sad to say,

but maybe I wasn't ready.
And maybe she wasn't either.

We believed in each other
that much.

Sometimes
no matter what happens.

We stay.

No matter how bad it hurts.

We stay.

Some people just speak to us
in ways we never imagined.

In ways
we'll never understand.

You quite don't know how
to let them go.

How to move on.

You stay.

Even if everything
is telling you

to leave.

There's no explanation
for it.

It's just something
we do.

PROPERLY LOVE

You can change your mind.

But you can't change
your heart.

You're going to love
who you're going to love.

Even if
the only thing that person brings you

is pain.

The heart gives you truth.
It gives you what you ***need***

and sometimes
not what you *want.*

Sometimes it gives you destruction.

Pain.
Suffering.

But in the end,
it is always for something.

For growth.

For a lesson.
For maturity.

For self-esteem.
The list can go on.

It attracts who it must.

It is there
to make you stronger.

It is there
to teach you

how to properly
love.

DON'T GO

I want you.

And I don't want
to put myself

in a position
to lose you.

In a position
 to lose us.

I want us to work out.
I don't

want to jeopardize
anything.

I don't
want to regret losing

the kind of love
I have stored for you.

I need you in my life.
Don't go.

I know everything will be
okay.

TOO MUCH CONTROL

She has a lot inside.

Too much.
Her small body

can't contain it.

Can't control
what it is she feels.

The fire.
Burns.

Too long.
All day.

All night.

It never ends.

It only grows stronger.

Larger.
Brighter.

I can see
it might be a problem.

It might be a blessing.
It is too early to tell.

Too late
to shut it off.

Too hard to contain.

To dull out
into the darkness.

I try to understand
but I cannot.

I try to make sense of it.
But it is harder to do.

I watch.
I set her free.

Encourage.

But I am very terrified
of what can happen.

It can go anyway.

Light.
Dark.

Heaven.

Hell.

I do not know.
No one does.

All we know is
that she has too much

inside of her.

Too much
to contain.

Too much
to control.

And witnessing it
is a beautiful

yet terrifying
thing to experience.

SOMEONE ONCE

Someone once told me
to not be afraid

of what the future holds.

To not be afraid
of letting go.

Of starting over
with someone new.

I think a lot of people
are afraid.

They are afraid
of the unknown.

Of the "what if."

Of change.
It's a hard pill to swallow.

To reset your entire life
and to start over again.

To redo
some of the things you've done.

To have to put time
into someone again.

Love.
Patience.

It can be exhausting,
I know.

But don't be afraid
of starting over.

Don't be afraid
of the outcome.

Of life on the other side
of comfort.

Don't be afraid
of moving on-of

being haunted
by your past.

Because fear is a motherfucker.
Fear will really hold you down.

It weighs heavy
on your chest

and will prevent you

from getting what you deserve.
So please.

Don't be afraid
of starting over.

Of taking your time
with someone new.

Don't be afraid
of change.

Of letting go
of the people

who keep doing you wrong.
The ones who keep

giving you stress.

The ones who keep
causing depression.

Who bring more darkness
than light.

Who always doubt you.
Who always have something

bad to say.

You don't need that type
of shit

in your life.

You don't need
to stay

if you don't want to.

ROBERT M. DRAKE

NUMBNESS

I know you feel alone.
I know you feel broken.

As if something is missing.
As if

you lost a piece
of yourself.

One you've needed
for the past several years.

I could see this in your eyes.
The way you look at people.

Looking far
into their eyes,

searching.

Trying to discover
that piece.

Digging into their souls
for a miracle.

For an answer.

I know you feel
out of place sometimes.

Out of yourself.
Like you don't belong.

No matter
who you're currently with.

I know it's deeper
than love.

Deeper than your friends
or family or even what you do

for a living.

I know this dilemma
begins with you.

Ends with you.
But you don't have

the slightest clue
on how to tackle it.

On how to pin point
the source of it—what

causes it.

It's hard.
I know.

And you wish
it would go away.

This feeling
of feeling heavy

yet empty.

This feeling of falling
yet not being able

to see where you're going
to crash land.

Or when
you're going to hit

solid grounds.

Some kind of comfort.
Stability, you know?

You're sad
aren't you?

And hell,
you don't even know why.

You have everything
going on for you.

And still,
you feel helpless.

You feel as if
you're not in control.

This feeling.
This web of numbness.

Of brokenness
just stays with you.

No matter how happy
you pretend to be.

No matter who you try
to express yourself to.

No matter who listens
and who doesn't.

It's hard to convince people
of what you're feeling.

Because you yourself
don't even fully understand why.

But I understand.

Depression is a motherfucker.

It creeps up on you
whenever it feels like it.

And it stays
as long as it wants.

As long as it needs.

Depression is a motherfucker.

A bastard not willing
to let you go.

Not willing
to walk away.

Not willing
to set you free.

Depression is a motherfucker.

It really is.
And it is really out to get you.

To destroy you.
To rain on you.

But you must be stronger
than that.

You must be willing
to fight back.

To try to not let it
get the best of you.

To try to not
give in.

Don't let it dictate your life.

Don't let it
tell you what to feel.

Depression is a motherfucker.

But you're a lot tougher
than you think.

OR NOT

Lover or not.
Friend or not.

In my life or not.

I hope one day
we find each other

in some distant future.

I hope one day
I run into you

by coincidence.

By accident.
Like you crossing the street

and I so happen
to look toward your direction

at the right time
and at the right moment

and say:

"There she goes.
The one who only

understood me.

It's a shame
it didn't work out.

A shame
we didn't spend more time together.

A shame
that some thing

so good
had to come to an end.

To a complete halt.
It's sad to think

we are not together anymore.
Sad to realize

how it all
fell apart

and we stood there
because we mutually felt

there was nothing
we could do about it.

I now understand.

*I now understand
how valuable she is.*

*I hope she's moved on.
I hope she's stronger*

than before.

*Happier.
Living her life
to the fullest.*

*Swimming in the ocean
of her deep heart.*

*I hope she's a different person.
A better version*

*of herself
than the one I used to know."*

It's sad to look back on things.
On certain little moments

that caused us
to go our separate ways.

It's sad to try to figure it out.
To understand

what it was exactly

that caused our doom.

And now,
I could only hope

that perhaps,
one day,

she too
sees me by accident

and she too
thinks the very same way

as I do.

The very same way
about us.

It's sad to say
but we let things end
too soon.

Too quickly.

The sun dawns
and the moon rises.

And it's a shame
we no longer

know each other.
It's a shame

we've become people
we used

to know.

AFTER IT ENDS

After everything
you've been through.

You deserve
to be free.

You deserve
to be appreciated.

To be loved
the same way
you love.

After everything
you've been through.

You deserve someone
just as rare as you.

Someone who sees
themselves in you.

Someone who understands
what sacrifice is about.

What putting the people
you love

before anyone is like.

After everything
you've been through.

All the pain
and bullshit relationships.

All the lies
and all the mind games

that have led you
to depression.

That have led you
to anxiety.

To too many
sleepless nights.

Isn't it time
you've had enough?

Isn't it time for you
to find someone real?

Someone who isn't
afraid to love?

Someone who isn't
going to fuck around

with your soul.

After everything you've been through.

Everything.

You deserve to let go.
To move on.

To start over.
You deserve to be

your own queen.
Your own king.

You deserve to survive.
To keep going.

And leave the heaviness aside.
You deserve people.

The ones
with the deepest hearts.

The ones
with the expanding souls.

You deserve so much more
than what they gave you.

You deserve

to love yourself.

To set your own
heart on fire.

To breathe at your own pace.

To let go
if you want to

let go.

And to love whom
you deserve to love.

After everything
you've been through.

You owe this
to yourself.

MY LIFE

Your smile saved me.

That's why I'm not
afraid of being vulnerable

with you.

Of being real
and honest with you.

You have given me life
in all parts

I thought
couldn't breathe.

And it was your smile.
From the moment

I saw it.

I knew
I wanted it

in my life.

AWARD SHOW 2

You always give
the people you love

something so important
that it gives them

the power
to destroy your heart.

To destroy
who you are.

You love that much.

You care that deeply.
You feel that close

to it all.

Everyone you meet
means something to you.

Long term
or not.

You are always willing
to love.
You are always willing

to lose
a piece of yourself.

And at the cost
of others.

And that's not necessarily
a bad thing.

You're a lover.
Not a sucker.

You just want everyone
to like you.

To appreciate you.
To call you when they need you

the most.

To depend on you
for anything.

And that means
a lot.

That speaks volumes
about the goodness

you have
within.

You're a good person
and you're soft like that.

And it's such
a beautiful thing to be.

I hope you never change.
I hope you're heart

never feels lonely.

I hope you never
experience fake love.

This is the part of you—you
need to hold on to.

The part of you—you
should be proud of.

The part of you—you
should keep sharing.

Stay beautiful, baby.

Your selflessness
is the rarest thing

in the world.

People like you

should be sitting
on a pedestal

near the sun.

People like you
should always deserve more

than that
of what

they receive.

FAIR TO DO SO

It's hard to believe
how fast someone

can switch up
on you.

Like one day
you're the most important

person
in the world.

And the next.

You're someone
they used to know.

This type of thing happens
all of the time.

It's unavoidable.
Sometimes people are going

to take you for granted.
Use you

for their own personal gain,
you know?

They're going to make it
seem as if

they need you.

As if
you're the only one

who can save them.

Help them
from their doom.

And no one knows why.
Not you.
Not them.

Not anyone.

No one knows why
these types of people

do this.

Why they abuse
on those

who really want to help them.
On those

who are really fucking

concerned.

And it's a shame
how they take the love

of others
and waste it.

They don't even consider
how much of a miracle

that is.

To have someone
risk themselves

to save you.
My god!

Some people can't sleep
at night

because they crave
to be held.

To be loved.
And in that same way.

While you have
these other types

of people
abusing the love of others.

And sleeping through the night
without a care

ignoring all of the destruction
they cause.

I'm telling you.

Some people
have it all backwards.

They have it all wrong.

They hurt those
who love them.

And love those
who never show them love.

In the end,
those people are doomed.

So please,
do not become one of them.

Do not waste
the love of others.

Do not waste
the love you have

within yourself.

And don't switch up
on people.

It's not fair
to do so.